If Not You, Then Who?

Noah's Treehouse

ISBN 978-1-951317-99-7

Published in the United States by Weeva, Inc.

First Printing, 2020

Story by David and Emberli Pridham with special assistance by Hayley Irvin of Weeva, Inc.

Creative direction by Emberli Pridham

Illustrations by Nadia Ronquillo

Graphic design by Rachel Bostick of Weeva, Inc.

Weeva

701 Brazos Street

Austin, TX 78735

www.weeva.com

Hello@Weeva.com

Available at bookstore.weeva.com

This book is dedicated to our children—Brooke, Noah, and Graham. You inspire us each and every day. Always remember to hold on to your dreams and never let go!

WELCOME TO NOAH'S TREEHOUSE!

After the release of our first book in this series, The Inventor in the Pink Pajamas, we received tremendous feedback. The response included hearing from children of all ages about how the message of our book—that no matter your age or background, you can do anything you put your mind to—inspired them. History is filled with stories of unlikely inventions and inventors. We decided to continue the series to reinforce this message and to bring more of these stories to the inventors and entrepreneurs of tomorrow.

Treehouse day was finally here! Noah felt like he had waited forever.

Now the wait was over. And the sooner they started building, the better. There was going to be a meteor shower tomorrow night, and Dad had promised Noah that they could watch it from the treehouse if they built it in time.

Noah buckled his tool belt, laced up his work boots, and raced downstairs, ready to get to work.

But Dad was still studying their plans. Oh no, Noah thought. Not more waiting!

The hard hat was invented in 1919 by E.W. Bullard. Bullard owned a factory in San Francisco that made mining and safety equipment.

When his son returned home from World War I, Bullard had the idea to make a new safety hat based off his son's army helmet. Bullard's design had a leather brim and was made out of steamed canvas and glue. He was awarded U.S. Patent 1,770,376 in 1930 for his safety hat.

When workers began building the Golden Gate Bridge in 1933, they wore Bullard's helmets. It became the first official "hard hat area" in the United States.

"Dad, is it time to go to the store?"
Noah asked.

"Hey there, sleepasaurus rex!" Dad said.
"Ready whenever you are."

"Let's go then!" Noah said. Treehouse day
had officially begun!

The first handheld calculator was invented at Texas Instruments by Jack Kilby, Jerry Merryman, and James Van Tassel in the 1970s.

Back then, calculators were large, heavy, and slow. TI's design was smaller, lighter, and faster. This was no easy feat, so the engineers split up the work. Kilby designed the output and power supply. Van Tassel built the keyboard, and Merryman worked on the memory and processor.

They were awarded U.S. Patent 3,819,921 in 1974 for their miniature electronic calculator (that was actually the size of a book).

What would your perfect treehouse look like?

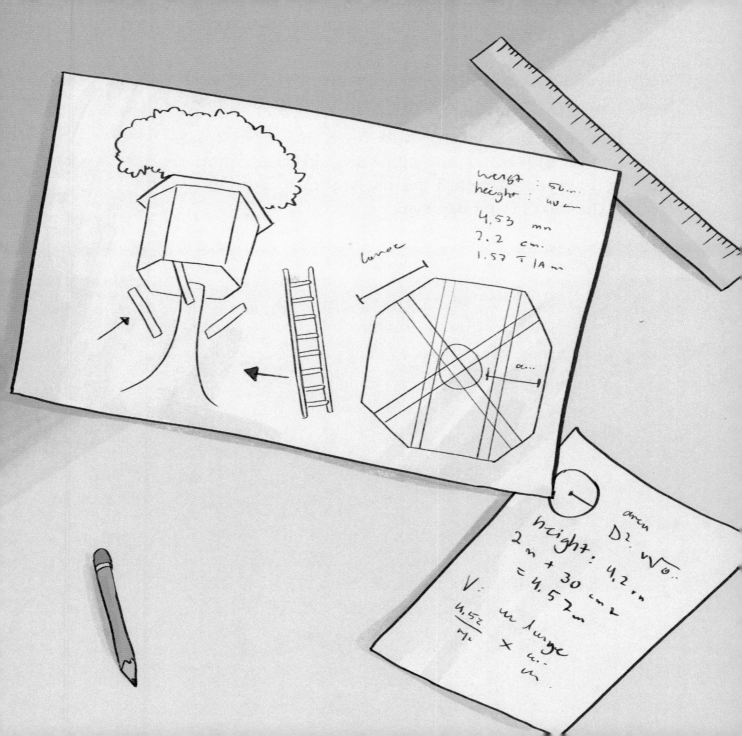

Noah loved going to the hardware store with Dad. It was a huge place filled with everything you could ever need to build anything.

As they wound their way up and down the aisles, Noah imagined all the things he and Dad could build together—a balloon-powered jetpack, a luxury doghouse. And of course, the best treehouse ever.

The shopping cart was invented in 1937 by Sylvan Goldman. Goldman owned a grocery store and wanted customers to be able to carry more groceries while they shopped.

After trying out different designs, he finally chose one that had a metal frame and two wire baskets. He received U.S. Patent 2,196,914 in 1938 for his folding basket carriage.

Goldman's shopping cart was not an instant success. Both men and women thought it looked like pushing a baby stroller. In fact, to get customers to use them, Goldman had to hire models to walk around his store showing how useful they could be!

One of Noah's favorite places in the hardware store was the paint aisle. He would watch with fascination as the paint mixer spun the different colors together to make new ones—reds and blues into deep purples, blues and yellows into lush greens.

This time, Noah decided to go with his favorite shade of blue.

Fred A. Schletz invented the paint mixer in 1933. Schletz owned three paint stores, and he invented a mixing machine to keep his paint fresh. He received U.S. Patent 2,022,526 in 1935 for his mixing machine.

Because of his money-saving invention, Schletz's stores were able to survive the Great Depression. Afterwards, demand for paint mixers soared, so Schletz sold his stores and began making paint mixers full-time.

Finally, the last item on the list: lumber for the floors, walls, and roof. Dad pushed the very full, very heavy cart all the way to the back of the store. OH NO! The lumber was all gone!

"Up there!" Noah said.

He had spotted what they needed—
all the way on the top shelf. How
would they ever get it down?

Noah heard the roar of a motor getting closer. He raced to the end of the aisle and waved to an employee driving a forklift.

"Can you help us?" Noah asked.

"Happy to!" the driver said. "It's no problem to take this up to the front of the store for you. That cart looks heavy!"

The forklift was invented in 1917 at the Clark Equipment Company. To help move heavy loads around the factory, employees added an engine and a seat to the company's lift trucks.

Clark wasn't planning to sell their Tructractors at first. When customers saw them in use and asked if they could buy one, the company changed its mind. In 1919, the Clark Tructractor Company was founded to produce the trucks full-time. They received U.S. Patent 1,707,428 in 1929 for their automobile lift truck, which became known as the Truclift.

Back at home, it was finally time to start building. While Dad and Grandpa worked on the floor for the treehouse, Noah moved the sand for the sandbox. But it was so heavy! There had to be an easier way...

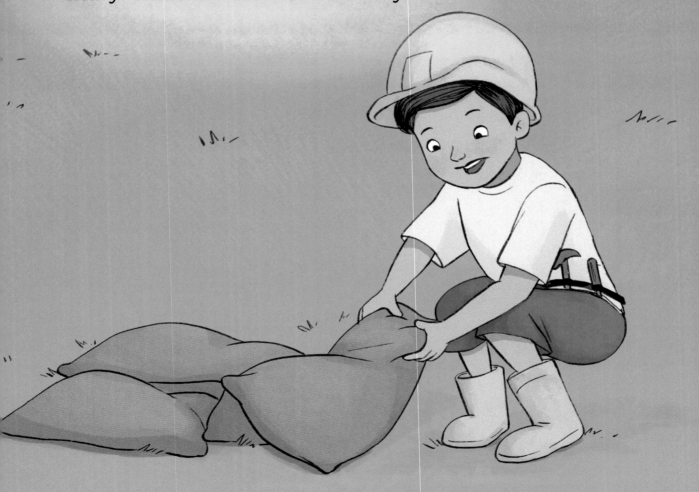

**Problem solved!
Back to work!**

Sounds of their bustling construction site now filled the backyard. There was the creak of the wagon wheels as they turned...

...and the buzzing of the power drills as Dad and Grandpa put together the walls.

Buzzzz. Buzzzz.

S. Duncan Black and Alonzo G. Decker founded the Black & Decker Manufacturing Company in 1910 in Baltimore, Maryland. They met in 1906 when they both worked at the Rowland Telegraph company. With $1200 between them, Black and Decker quit their jobs and started their own machine shop.

At first, Black and Decker built machines for making milk bottle caps and dipping candy. Eventually, they started making tools. In 1917, Black and Decker invented the tool that would make them famous: the cordless, trigger-switch power drill.

But suddenly the buzzing stopped! OH NO! What happened?

Black and Decker's power drill wasn't the first, but it was the best version yet: easier to hold, easier to use, and easier to transport. They received U.S. Patent 1,245,860 in 1917 for their electrically-driven tool.

Other cool Black and Decker inventions...

1962: Cordless hedge trimmers (U.S. Patent 3212188). Black and Decker began making lawn tools in 1957, but they really changed the game in 1962 when they invented the first cordless outdoor tool.

1975: Cordless, handheld vacuums (U.S. Patent 4,011,624). You might know it as a Dustbuster, but this device was invented to help astronauts on the Apollo space mission take core samples from the moon!

Noah remembered Dad's extension cord and had an idea. He fetched it from the garage and brought the cord to Dad.

"Dad, will this help?" Noah asked.

"Great idea, Noah!" Dad said.

Buzzzz. Buzzzz.
Success!

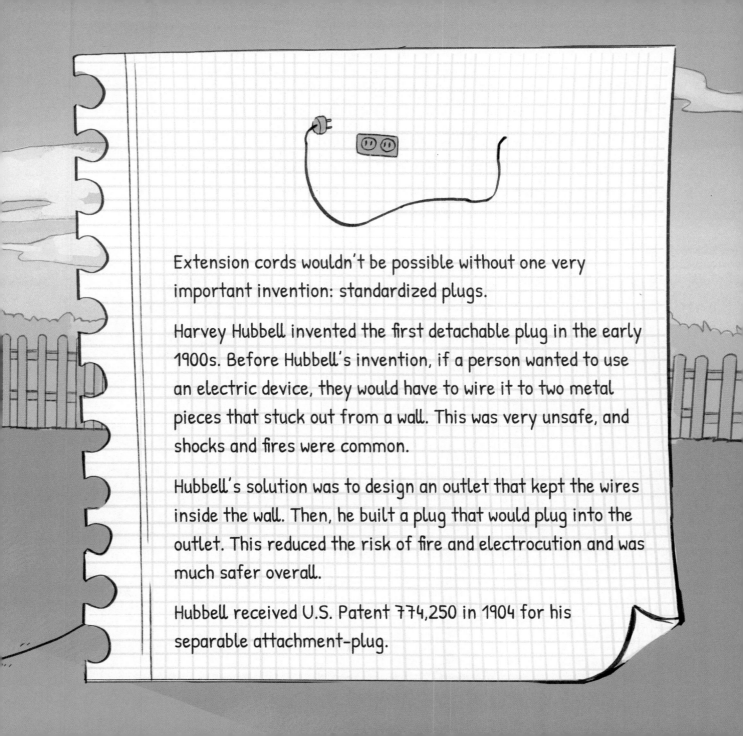

Extension cords wouldn't be possible without one very important invention: standardized plugs.

Harvey Hubbell invented the first detachable plug in the early 1900s. Before Hubbell's invention, if a person wanted to use an electric device, they would have to wire it to two metal pieces that stuck out from a wall. This was very unsafe, and shocks and fires were common.

Hubbell's solution was to design an outlet that kept the wires inside the wall. Then, he built a plug that would plug into the outlet. This reduced the risk of fire and electrocution and was much safer overall.

Hubbell received U.S. Patent 774,250 in 1904 for his separable attachment-plug.

And then the craziest thing happened—it started raining. Dad, Grandpa, and Noah had just enough time to cover everything up before it was all soaked.

Noah had a flash of fear. What if they didn't finish the treehouse in time for the meteor shower?

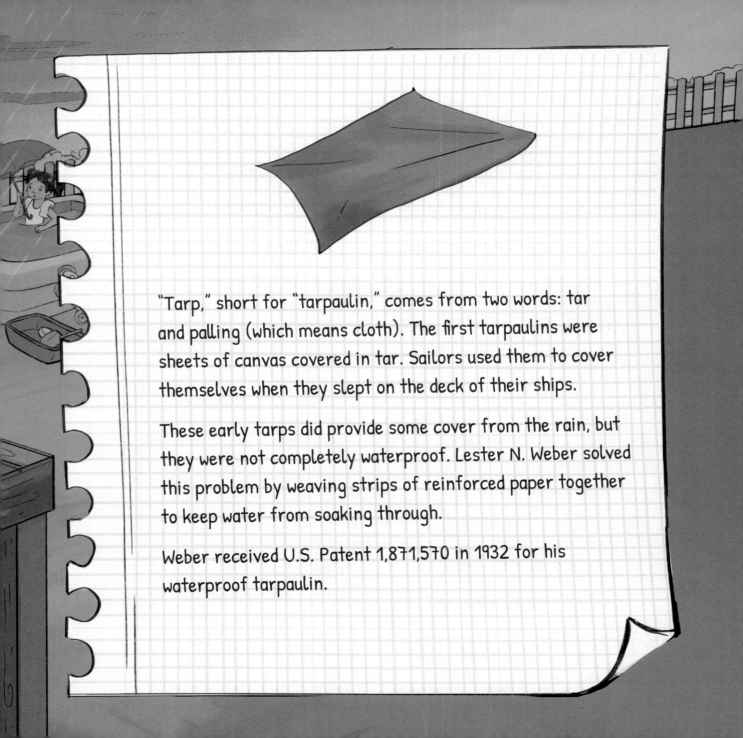

"Tarp," short for "tarpaulin," comes from two words: tar and palling (which means cloth). The first tarpaulins were sheets of canvas covered in tar. Sailors used them to cover themselves when they slept on the deck of their ships.

These early tarps did provide some cover from the rain, but they were not completely waterproof. Lester N. Weber solved this problem by weaving strips of reinforced paper together to keep water from soaking through.

Weber received U.S. Patent 1,871,570 in 1932 for his waterproof tarpaulin.

What's a useful tool you could create?

But Noah persisted.

"I'm not going to let a little rain get in my way," he thought. "It's time for Project Backup Plan."

That night, Noah pulled his covers over his head and got to work on his master plan...

Walter Hunt was an American engineer from New York. Hunt was a very prolific inventor and invented many items we still use today. Some of his most famous inventions include fountain pens, sewing machines, inkstands, and ice plows.

Noah was up bright and early the next morning and rushed to tell his still-sleepy family about Project Backup Plan.

"I thought of everything!" he said. "Even Gus Gus has a job.

Here, we can pin on these tags so no one forgets their part of the plan."

"Ruff!" Gus Gus said. But Noah knew he meant, "Let's get this treehouse party started!"

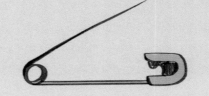

Hunt's best-known invention is the safety pin. One day, while trying to figure out a way to pay back $15 to a friend, Hunt twisted a piece of wire into a pin. His design was based on an earlier version, but Hunt added a coiled spring on one end to make it easier to use.

Hunt received U.S Patent 6,281 in 1849 for his dress-pin. Not realizing the potential of his invention, Hunt sold the patent for $400. Hunt had enough money to pay back his friend and still had some left over, but the company he sold the patent to made much more.

Step 1: Mom and Dad build the railing.

Step 2: Grandpa puts the rope ladder together.

Self-locking screws were invented by William Arthur Purtell in 1937. In addition to being an inventor, Purtell also served in World War I, spent ten years as a salesman, started his own company, and was even elected to the U.S. Senate!

Purtell's invention aimed to solve a common problem: the fact that screws loosen over time. Purtell's design angled the threads of the screw so they would lock into place. As a result, self-locking screws won't move unless a screwdriver or other tool is used.

Purtell received U.S. Patent 2,177,003 in 1939 for his self-locking screw.

Step 3: Noah, Brooke, and Gus Gus finish painting.

An oscillating fan turns from side to side as it blows air. Like many inventions, it wasn't the first of its kind, but it did improve on earlier versions.

The electric fan was invented in 1882 by Schuyler Skaats Wheeler. In 1891, Philip Diehl improved on Wheeler's device by adding a motor and attaching the fan to the ceiling. Diehl received U.S. Patent 550,042 in 1895 for his electric fan.

Diehl's first improvement to his fan was to add a light. Then, in 1904, he added a split-ball joint, which allowed the fan to change directions. This became the first oscillating fan.

Step 4: Move in supplies.

An assembly line is a way to quickly produce machines with many parts, like cars or electronics. Items move from station to station with a new part added at every stop. The first American carmaker to use an assembly line was Ransom Olds in 1901.

In 1913, Henry Ford began using a moving assembly line at his factory. Ford added a conveyor belt so the cars moved from station to station while the employees stayed in one place. Ford's moving assembly line was faster, cheaper, and safer, and other carmakers soon began using it at their factories.

And voila—the treehouse was done! And just in time, too. The sun was starting to dip below the horizon. The meteor shower would be starting soon.

But there was one last surprise for Noah...

He couldn't believe it. A treehouse AND a telescope all in one weekend? What more could a kid ask for?

The telescope was invented in 1608 in the Netherlands. Glasses-maker Hans Lipperhey was the first to apply for a patent for his kijker ("looker").

A few weeks later, another glasses-maker named Jacob Metius tried to patent his device for "seeing faraway things as though nearby." Both applications were denied because the devices were so similar.

Metius received a small amount of money, but Lipperhey's invention quickly spread through Europe. Astronomer Galileo Galilei saw Lipperhey's telescope and built his own version that could see things even farther away.

Galileo then turned his telescope to the stars. He observed the Milky Way, Saturn's rings, and Jupiter's moons.

As Noah watched the first of many stars shoot across the night sky, all he could think was...

Best. Treehouse Day. Ever.

THINGS TO KNOW ABOUT PATENTS

WHAT IS A PATENT?

A patent is a kind of **intellectual property.** The person who holds it can prevent others from making, using, or selling their invention for a set amount of time.

Intellectual property is a "creation of the mind." Inventions, books, drawings, and brand names are all forms of intellectual property.

WHAT CAN BE PATENTED?

Any device or discovery that uses a new process, machine, or material can be patented. Improvements to existing devices and discoveries can also be patented.

Laws of nature and abstract ideas cannot be patented. To be granted a patent, the applicant must include a complete description of their device or discovery.

ARE THERE DIFFERENT KINDS OF PATENTS?

Yes! Utility patents protect the way a device is used, made, or operated. Design patents protect its appearance.

HOW LONG DO PATENTS LAST?

Utility patents are granted for 20 years from the date the application is filed. Design patents are granted for 14 years.

WHO CAN APPLY FOR A PATENT?

Anyone! According to patent law, an inventor (or someone who is helping them) may apply for a patent for their work.

FUN FACTS ABOUT PATENTS

In 1809, Mary Dixon Kies became the first American woman to receive a patent. She invented a new way to weave straw, silk, and thread to make hats.

Abraham Lincoln is currently the only US president to hold a patent. He created a device to lift boats over sandbars, but it was never built.

The longest US patent (US 20,070,224,201) has 7,154 pages!

TIMELINE OF INVENTIONS

1608: Hans Lipperhey invents the telescope in the Netherlands.

1904: Harvey Hubbell receives U.S Patent 774,250 for his separable attachment-plug.

1930: Edward Bullard receives U.S. Patent 1770376 for his safety hat.

1917: Employees at the Clark Equipment Company build the Tructractor, the first forklift.

1895: Philip Diehl invents the electric fan.

1917: Black and Decker receive U.S. Patent 1,245,860 for their electric power drill.

1913: Henry Ford uses the first moving assembly line at his car factory in Michigan.

1933: Fred A. Schletz is awarded U.S Patent 2,022,526 for his mixing machine.

1974: Merryman, Van Tassel, and Kirby receive U.S. Patent 3,819,921 for their miniature electronic calculator.

1938: Sylvan Goldman builds the first shopping cart in Oklahoma City.

1937: William Arthur Purtell patents self-locking screws.

1975: Black and Decker patents the first handheld vacuum, the Dustbuster.

1932: Lester Weber is awarded U.S. Patent 1,871,570 for his waterproof tarpaulin.

1962: Black and Decker receive U.S. Patent 4,011,624 for their cordless hedge trimmers.

IF YOU LIKED "NOAH'S TREEHOUSE" AND WANT TO GO ON MORE
ADVENTURES WITH BROOKE, NOAH, AND BABY GRAHAM, CHECK OUT
THESE OTHER TITLES FROM THE "IF NOT YOU, THEN WHO?" SERIES:

Join our mailing list at **IfNotYouBooks.com** to be the first to know
about new releases and special promotions, and be sure to leave a
review for other young inventors!

We can't wait to hear from you!

David & Emberli